Saturn

Uranus

Neptune

The Sun and Other Stars

Editor in chief: Paul A. Kobasa
Supplementary Publications: Jeff De La Rosa,
    Christine Sullivan, Scott Thomas, Kristina Vaicikonis,
    Marty Zwikel
Research: Mike Barr, Cheryl Graham, Jacqueline Jasek,
    Barbara Lightner, Loranne Shields
Graphics and Design: Kathy Creech, Sandra Dyrlund,
    Tom Evans, Isaiah Sheppard, Brenda Tropinski
Permissions: Janet Peterson
Indexing: David Pofelski
Pre-Press and Manufacturing: Carma Fazio, Anne Fritzinger,
    Steven Hueppchen, Tina Ramirez
Writer: Lori Meek Schuldt

World Book, Inc.
233 N. Michigan Avenue
Chicago, IL 60601
U.S.A.

The Library of Congress has cataloged an earlier printing of
this title as follows:
The sun and other stars. --2nd ed.
    p. cm. --(World Book's solar system & space exploration
library)
    Summary: "Introduction to the sun and other stars, providing
to primary and intermediate grade students information on their
features and exploration. Includes fun facts, glossary, resource
list and index"--Provided by publisher.
    Includes bibliographical references and index.
    ISBN-13: 978-0-7166-9521-9
    ISBN-10: 0-7166-9521-9
    1. Sun--Juvenile literature. 2. Stars--Juvenile literature.
I. World Book, Inc.
QB521.5.S86 2007
523.7--dc22
                                    2006030047

This printing:
ISBN: 978-0-7166-9532-5 (The sun and Other Stars)
ISBN: 978-0-7166-9522-6 (set)

Printed in China

2 3 4 5 6 7 8 09 08 07

**For information about other World Book publications,
visit our Web site at http://www.worldbookonline.com or call
1-800-WORLDBK (967-5325).**

**For information about sales to schools and libraries,
call 1-800-975-3250 (United States);
1-800-837-5365 (Canada).**

Picture Acknowledgments: Front Cover: NASA/SOHO/ESA; Back Cover: NASA/SOHO/ESA; Royal Swedish
Academy of Sciences; © David A. Hardy, Photo Researchers; Inside Back Cover: © John Gleason, Celestial Images.

© David Malin, Anglo-Australian Observatory 35; Digitized Sky Survey/STScI 29; NASA 13; NASA/CXC/SAO 53;
NASA/CXC/SAO/STScI/JPL-Caltech 51; NASA/Harvard Smithsonian Center for Astrophysics 47; NASA/JPL 43;
NASA/SOHO/ESA 3, 11, 23, 45; NASA/STScI 59; NASA/STScI/AURA 27, 31; NASA/STScI/AURA/AVL 57;
NASA/STScI/ESA 33, 41; © Lynette Cook, Photo Researchers 49; © David A. Hardy, Photo Researchers 55; © Steve
Munsinger, Photo Researchers 25; © SPL/Photo Researchers 21 (top), 37; © Frank Zullo, Photo Researchers 17;
Royal Swedish Academy of Sciences 19; U.S. Naval Research Laboratory 21 (bottom).

Illustrations: Inside Front Cover: WORLD BOOK illustration by Steve Karp; Back Cover: WORLD BOOK
illustration by Rob Wood; World Book illustration by Precision Graphics 7; World Book illustrations by Roberta
Polfus 1, 9, 15; WORLD BOOK illustration by Rob Wood 61.

Astronomers use different kinds of photos to learn about objects in space—such as planets. Many photos show an
object's natural color. Other photos use false colors. Some false-color images show types of light the human eye
cannot normally see. Others have colors that were changed to highlight important features. When appropriate,
the captions in this book state whether a photo uses natural or false colors.

WORLD BOOK'S

SOLAR SYSTEM & SPACE EXPLORATION LIBRARY

The Sun and Other Stars

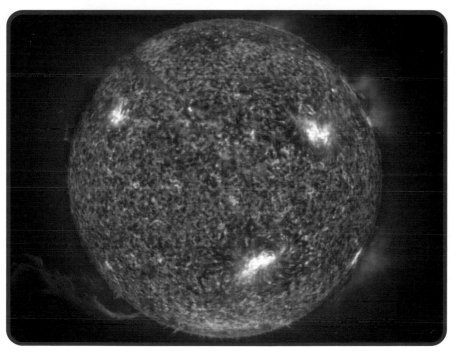

SECOND EDITION

WORLD BOOK

a Scott Fetzer company
Chicago
www.worldbookonline.com

J

Contents

THE SUN

If a word is printed in **bold letters that look like this,** that word's meaning is given in the glossary on page 63.

OTHER STARS

Where Is the Sun?

The sun is the **star** closest to Earth. The sun is, on average, about 93 million miles (150 million kilometers) from Earth. Sunlight, which travels at 186,282 miles (299,792 kilometers) per second, takes about 8 minutes to reach Earth.

The sun is a huge, glowing ball at the center of our **solar system.** It is the only star in our solar system. Earth and the other **planets** of our solar system travel around the sun. Other objects, such as **asteroids** and **comets,** also **orbit** the sun.

The sun is about 25,000 **light-years** from the center of our **galaxy,** the Milky Way Galaxy. It takes the sun about 250 million years to revolve around the center of the Milky Way.

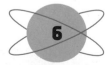

Solar System Locator

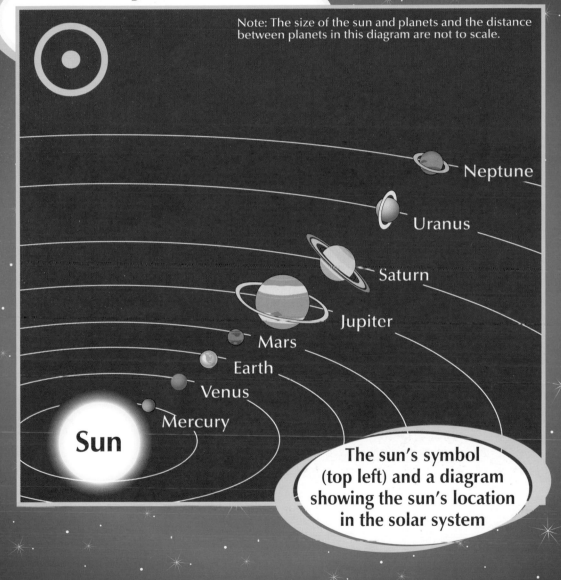

Note: The size of the sun and planets and the distance between planets in this diagram are not to scale.

Neptune

Uranus

Saturn

Jupiter

Mars

Earth

Venus

Mercury

Sun

The sun's symbol (top left) and a diagram showing the sun's location in the solar system

How Big Is the Sun?

To us, the sun seems huge, and it is. But, for a **star,** it is average-sized and fairly usual.

Still, the sun is by far the largest object in our **solar system.** The sun's **radius** is about 432,000 miles (695,500 kilometers). That is about 109 times as large as Earth's radius.

To picture how these sizes compare, imagine Earth as roughly the size of an adult and the sun as the size of a tall building. If Earth's radius were the height of a person, then the sun's radius would be about the height of a 60-story skyscraper. The sun is so large that in a drawing to scale that shows both Earth and the sun, we can only show a small portion of the sun. Otherwise the drawing would have to show the Earth at a size too tiny to notice.

The **mass** of the sun is about 333,000 times as great as the mass of Earth.

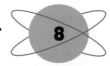

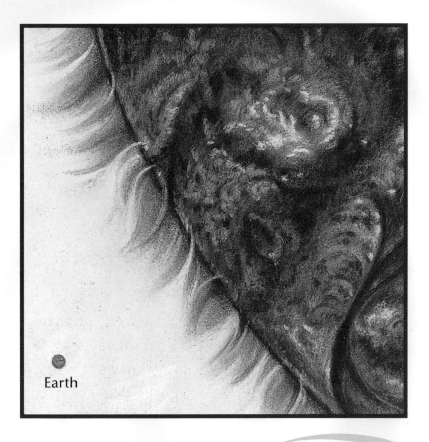

Earth

An artist's drawing comparing the size of the sun and Earth

How Hot Is the Sun?

The sun is extremely hot. The outer part that we see has a temperature of about 10,000 °F (5500 °C). That's more than 50 times hotter than the temperature at which water boils!

But **astronomers** express the sun's temperature in another way. They measure temperatures for the sun and other **stars** in a metric unit called the **Kelvin** (abbreviated K). The Kelvin scale starts at absolute zero. Scientists think that at this temperature, **atoms** and **molecules** have the least possible energy. On the Fahrenheit and Celsius scales, absolute zero is equal to -459.67 °F and -273.15 °C, respectively. From absolute zero, or 0 K, the scale rises by units of 1 Kelvin, which is equal to 1.8 Fahrenheit degrees or 1 Celsius degree.

Thus, the solar surface has a temperature of about 5800 K. However, temperatures in the sun's **core** reach more than 15 million K.

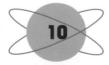

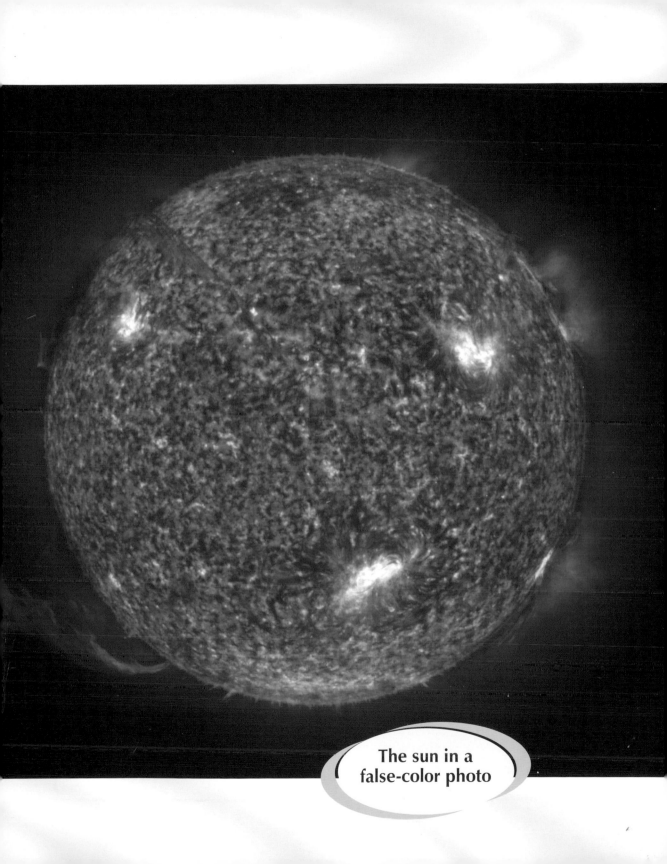

The sun in a false-color photo

From Where Does the Sun's Energy Come?

The sun's energy comes from **nuclear fusion reactions** of **hydrogen** atoms that occur deep inside the sun's **core.**

An **atom** is one of the basic units that make up **matter,** and an element is a substance made up of only one kind of atom. The word *nuclear* refers to the nucleus, the center of an atom. In a fusion reaction, the nuclei of two lightweight elements fuse, or join together, to form the nucleus of a heavier element. The lighter hydrogen atoms in the sun continually crash into one another and fuse, making larger atoms of the heavier element **helium.** This fusion reaction releases great amounts of energy.

The sun releases this energy in two ways. The first and most plentiful type of energy the sun sends out includes the visible light we see from the sun and the heat rays that warm our **planet.** The second kind of energy that the sun sends out is made up mostly of electrically charged atomic particles.

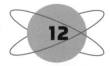

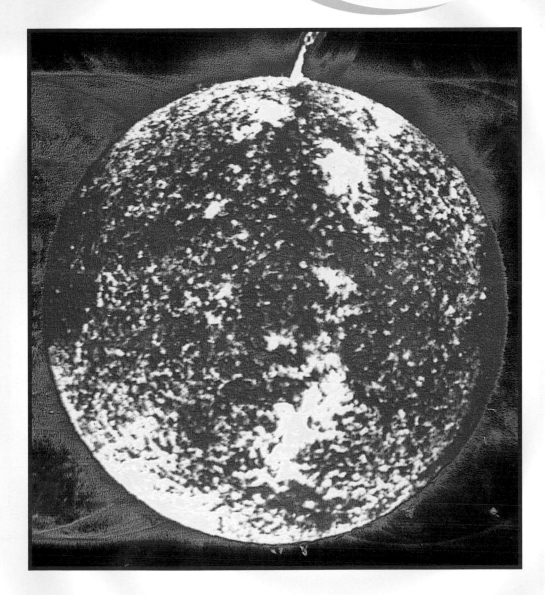

The sun's radiation is shown in a false-color image

What Makes Up the Sun?

The sun is made up mostly of the chemical element **hydrogen.** The other element that makes up a large portion of the sun's **mass** is **helium.** There also are small amounts of a few other elements in the sun.

The sun is so hot that none of its **matter** exists in either solid or liquid form. All of the sun's matter is in the form of a gas or another form called **plasma.** When a gas is heated to a very hot temperature, the **atoms** making up the gas come apart. This leaves electrically charged atoms—called **ions**—and electrically charged atomic particles—called **electrons.** Scientists call the form of matter made up of these electrically charged ions and electrons plasma. Some of the elements that make up the sun are in gas form, but much of the solar matter exists in plasma form.

The sun consists of several zones, or layers. At the center of the sun is the **core.** Energy flows outward from the core through the radiative zone. The convection zone, a layer of violently churning gases, extends from the radiative zone to the sun's surface.

A diagram showing the sun's layers

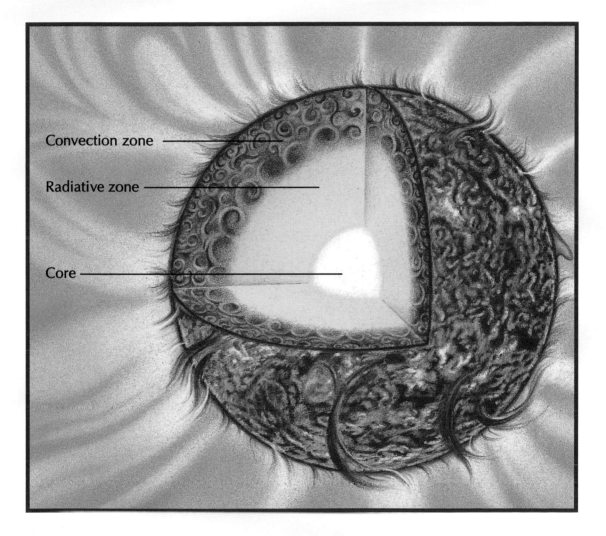

Convection zone

Radiative zone

Core

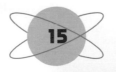

What Is the Sun's Atmosphere Like?

The sun's **atmosphere** has several layers. The photosphere, the lowest part of the atmosphere of the sun, rises from the **star's** surface. This layer sends out the sunlight that we see on Earth.

Above the photosphere is the chromosphere. Temperatures rise dramatically in this layer of the sun's atmosphere.

The layer above the chromosphere is the transition region. It is so named because it is the region where a transition, or change, occurs between the chromosphere and the next layer of the sun, the corona. Temperatures in the transition region are much higher than in the chromosphere.

The outermost layer, the corona, is the hottest layer. The corona is so hot that it continually expands outward into space. This flow of coronal gas into space is known as the solar wind.

The glow of the sun's corona can be seen beyond the moon's edge

The moon in front of the sun during an eclipse. The sun's corona is shown in false color.

WARNING: Never stare directly at the sun. Even during an eclipse, when the sun can look darkened, the sun's direct rays can damage your eyes very badly.

What Types of Events Happen Within the Sun's Atmosphere?

The sun has a **magnetic field.** This magnetic field can rise up through the convection zone and erupt into the sun's **atmosphere.** This causes **sunspots, solar flares,** and **coronal mass ejections.**

Sunspots are dark, circular features on the solar surface. Areas where sunspots occur are known as active regions. The number of sunspots and the areas of the sun on which sunspots appear vary over a period of about 11 years. This period is known as the sunspot cycle.

A solar flare is a sudden brightening of a part of the solar atmosphere that releases a tremendous amount of magnetic energy. A solar flare causes a large increase in the temperature of the corona, to about 10 million K, and sometimes higher.

When large amounts of material from the corona erupt into space it is called a coronal mass ejection. These ejections occur when a large piece of the magnetic field erupts from the sun. This causes some of the corona to eject, creating a large cloud of gas.

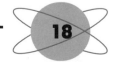

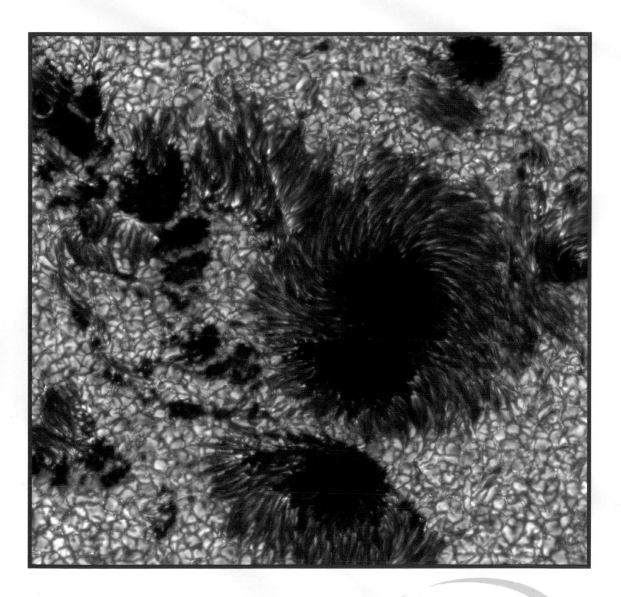

Sunspots in a
false-color photo

How Do Scientists Study the Sun?

For hundreds of years, scientists have used a variety of tools and methods to study the sun.

The first telescopes were made in the early 1600's. Within a few years, scientists, such as the **astronomer** Galileo (*GAL uh LAY oh* or *GAL uh LEE oh*), were using early telescopes to study the **star** at the center of our **solar system.** Telescopes became bigger and better over the centuries. Eventually, special devices were developed—filters for the telescope and eye protection for the **astronomer**—to keep astronomers from damaging their eyes when observing the sun.

Solar observers have been taking photographs of the sun since 1858. In the late 1800's, an instrument called the spectroheliograph was developed to allow astronomers to photograph the sun in different colors of the **spectrum,** a band of visible light or other kind of **radiation** arranged in order of wavelength. Such photos revealed that the sun's inner **atmosphere** was layered.

In the 1960's, scientists found that the surface of the sun vibrates. This discovery allowed scientists to study the sun's interior through these solar vibrations.

George Ellery Hale, using the spectroheliograph he invented (left), and a spectroheliograph image

How Are Satellites Used to Study the Sun ?

Since the 1960's, scientists have used **satellites** to study the sun. The United States National Aeronautics and Space Administration (NASA) has launched many spacecraft for this purpose. For example, NASA launched the Solar Maximum Mission Satellite in 1980.

In 1994, the space **probe** Ulysses—launched by NASA and the European Space Agency (ESA)—became the first craft to observe the sun from an **orbit** that carried it over the sun's polar regions. And, NASA and the ESA also maintain the Solar and Heliospheric Observatory (SOHO). This orbiting solar telescope, launched in 1995, takes images of the sun every 10 to 15 minutes.

NASA launched a new mission to observe the sun in 2006. STEREO, for *Solar Terrestrial Relations Observatory*, will use two separate satellites to study **coronal mass ejections** (see page 18) in three dimensions. These eruptions disturb Earth's **magnetic field,** sometimes producing a magnetic storm. These storms can damage orbiting satellites and spacecraft and even interfere with electrical equipment on the ground. Scientists hope to be better able to predict these storms in the future.

An artist's drawing of the Solar and Heliospheric Observatory (SOHO)

How Old Is the Sun and When Might It Burn Out?

The sun is about 4.6 billion years old. That is also the approximate age of the **solar system.**

Scientists think the sun's formation began when part of a huge, slowly spinning cloud of dust and gas became denser than the region that surrounded it. The **gravity** of this dense region caused the cloud to shrink. The shrinking caused the gas in the center to compress into a ball, which made the gas hotter. Eventually, the center of the ball became hot enough and dense enough for **nuclear fusion** (see page 12) to begin, and the ball became a **star,** our sun.

The sun has enough **hydrogen** in its **core** to continue radiating energy as it does today for another 5 billion years. Once that hydrogen is gone, the sun will become larger and brighter for a time. In this phase, it will be known as a red giant (see page 46). Eventually, the sun's outer layers will drift into space. The remaining core, called a white dwarf, will slowly fade to become a faint, cool object known as a black dwarf (see page 48).

An artist's drawing of a red giant (left) and a white dwarf (upper right)

What Is a Star?

Stars are shining objects in space. Most stars are made of gas and an electrically charged, gaslike substance known as **plasma.** Stars vary in size, but most stars produce a tremendous amount of energy. This energy is mostly in the form of light and heat.

There are many types of stars. About 75 percent of all stars are members of a binary system. A binary system is a pair of closely spaced stars that **orbit** each other. Types of stars include red and blue giants and supergiants and dwarfs of various colors.

Stars are plentiful to see in the night sky from Earth. There are about 6,000 stars that can be seen from Earth without using binoculars or a telescope. So, at any given time, you could see a maximum of about 3,000 stars. Stars are not spread out evenly in space. They are sometimes found in such formations as star clusters (large groups of stars held together by their gravitational attraction to one another). Stars and star clusters are grouped into huge structures called **galaxies.** The sun, the star at the center of our **solar system,** is in the Milky Way Galaxy. This galaxy has more than 100 billion stars.

A star cluster in a
natural-color photo

How Far Away Are the Stars?

The **star** closest to Earth is the sun. The sun is, on average, about 93 million miles (150 million kilometers) away from Earth. After the sun, the next closest star to our **solar system** is Proxima Centauri, which is more than 25 trillion miles (40 trillion kilometers) from the sun. This distance is so great that it takes 4.2 years for light to travel between Proxima Centauri and the sun. Thus, scientists say that the two stars are 4.2 **light-years** apart.

This will give you some idea of the distances in space. Imagine you had a magic car that could travel in space. If your car could travel continuously at 55 miles (89 kilometers) per hour, it would take about 30 weeks to travel to Earth's moon. It might take 50 years to travel to Venus, 200 years to travel to the sun, and 7,500 years to travel to distant Pluto. Proxima Centauri is so distant, it would take over 500 million years to travel there in your magic car.

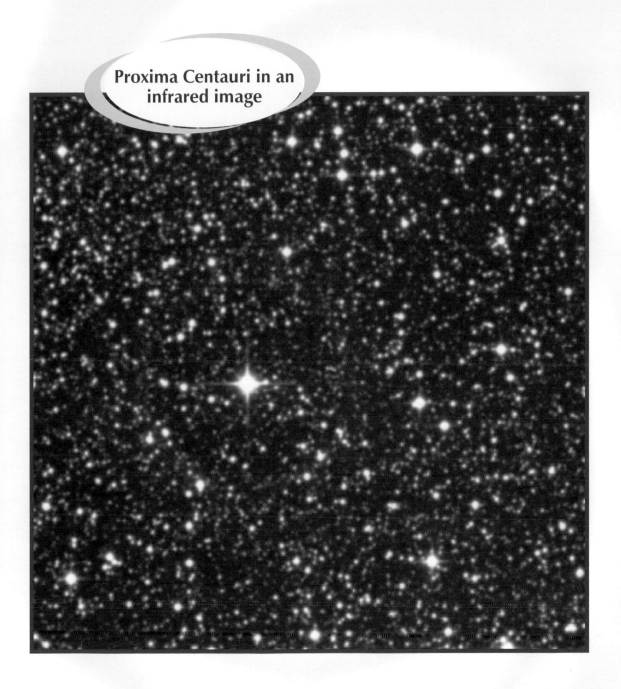

Proxima Centauri in an infrared image

What Do Stars Look Like?

If you want to imagine what a **star** looks like up close, imagine the sun. The sun is a fairly normal type of star, and most stars resemble it. Like the sun, most other stars are shaped like a ball and are bright and glowing. The reason stars other than our sun look like small points of light to us is that they are so far away from Earth.

Stars can be very bright in the night sky or very faint. How bright a star appears to us depends to some extent on its distance from Earth, but it also depends on the star's surface temperature and its size. If two stars have the same surface temperature but are different sizes, the bigger star will give off more light. But, if two stars are the same size but have different temperatures, the hotter star will give off more light.

Stars come in different colors. A star's color depends on its surface temperature. Stars that look red are the least hot, those that look yellow—such as the sun—are hotter, and those that look blue are the hottest.

Not all stars are bright and glowing like our sun. For instance, stars that have spent all of their fuel, such as white dwarfs (see page 48), do not shine much at all.

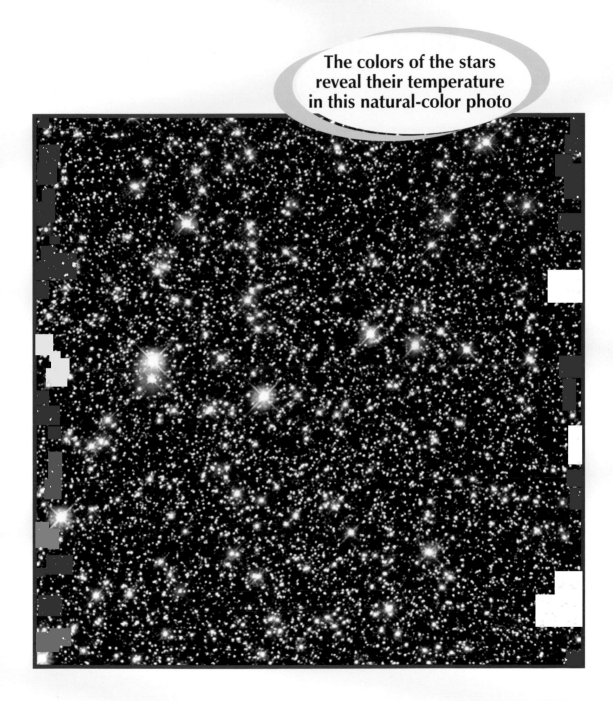

The colors of the stars reveal their temperature in this natural-color photo

How Big Are Stars?

The largest **stars,** called supergiants, can have a **radius** of about 650 million miles (1 billion kilometers). That is approximately 1,500 times greater than the sun's radius.

Astronomers classify the sun as a dwarf. Dwarf stars are not all small, but scientists call them "dwarfs" to distinguish them from much larger "giants."

Astronomers measure the size of stars in comparison to the sun's radius. For example, the supergiant star Antares has a radius about 700 times larger than the sun's radius. Thus, astronomers would say that Antares is roughly 700 solar radii (*radii* is the plural of radius). But Proxima Centauri, which is smaller than the sun, measures 0.145 solar radius.

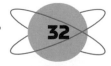

Comparing Star Size

A red dwarf—
usually from
between $\frac{1}{12}$ to $\frac{1}{2}$
times smaller
than the sun

The sun—
a yellow
dwarf star

A supergiant star—
can be about 1,500
times larger than
the sun

A drawing comparing
some types of stars
by their size

What Makes Up Stars?

The sun and most other **stars** are huge balls of hot gas and **plasma.** Most of a star's **mass** is composed of the chemical element **hydrogen.** Nearly all of the rest of the mass is made up of the chemical element **helium.** Small amounts of a few other elements make up the remaining mass.

A star forms when one part of a huge, swirling cloud of gas and dust in space becomes denser than the surrounding region. Because of the force of its own **gravity,** the cloud begins to collapse inward and shrink into a ball, spinning faster and faster. The object starts to make heat and becomes very hot. When the center of the object gets hot enough, it becomes a star.

A huge, star-forming cloud shown in a natural-color photo

Why Do Stars Shine?

Stars shine because they give off energy in the form of light. Most of this energy is produced through a process called a **nuclear fusion reaction** deep inside the star's **core.**

In the core, the centers, or nuclei, of **hydrogen** atoms continually crash into one another. When they collide, the nuclei fuse (join together) to form the nucleus of a heavier element, **helium.** This nuclear fusion reaction releases great amounts of energy. In the process, the star gets very hot and gives off light.

Stars shine all day and night, but during the day, the sun's bright light overpowers the faint light from other stars. We can see these other stars only at night when the sky is dark and clear.

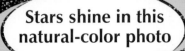

Stars shine in this natural-color photo

How Are Stars Classified?

   Astronomers classify (or group) **stars** by various characteristics. Such characteristics include size and **mass** (often measured in comparison to the sun).

   The charts at right show other ways to classify stars: color and surface temperature, and luminosity, or brightness. The spectral (color) classes in the first chart have letters assigned based upon a star's surface temperature. The letters assigned are, from hottest to coolest, O, B, A, F, G, K, M, and L. In addition, each of the class O through L is divided into types numbered 0 through 9. The hottest stars in a spectral class are assigned 0 and the coolest stars 9.

   Stars are further organized from brightest to least bright with these designations: Ia, Ib, II, III, IV, and V.

   These designations allow us to compare stars. For instance, the sun belongs to the class G2V, meaning it is a dwarf star (V) in the yellow (G) **spectrum** that is relatively hot (2). The star Alpha Centauri is also a G2V. So, despite apparent differences, we know that these two stars share some basic traits.

Classifying Stars

Color Classification	
O	Hottest blue stars
B	Hot blue stars
A	Blue/blue-white stars
F	White stars
G	Yellow stars
K	Orange-red stars
M	Red stars
L	Coolest red stars

Spectral class

Hottest stars

Coolest stars

Luminosity Classification	
Ia	Bright supergiants
Ib	Supergiants
II	Bright giants
III	Giants
IV	Subgiants
V	Main sequence or dwarf

Brightest stars

Faintest stars

The chart at the top of this page shows a classification system based upon the color of a star, which is related to a star's surface temperature. The chart at the bottom of this page gives a classification system based upon a star's brightness.

How Hot Are Stars?

   Stars are very, very hot! **Astronomers** measure star temperatures in a metric unit called the **Kelvin** (abbreviated K).

   Core temperatures for stars can range from about 10 million K to nearly 10 billion K. At the high end of the range are collapsing stars that are about to produce supernova explosions (see page 50).

   Surface temperatures also vary for stars. Red stars have a surface temperature that ranges from about 2500 K to 3500 K. The sun and other yellow stars have surface temperatures of about 5500 K. Blue stars range from about 10,000 to 50,000 K in surface temperature.

How Old Are Stars?

Most **stars** are from about 1 billion to 10 billion years old. Stars, like people, have life cycles. Stars are born, they pass through several stages of life, and they finally die. Some stars end their lives by slowly fading. Others spectacularly explode. The stage in a star's life during which it gets nearly all its energy from **nuclear fusion reactions** involving hydrogen in its **core** is called the **main-sequence phase.**

The life cycles of stars follow three types of patterns, depending on whether the star's starting **mass,** measured in comparison to the sun, is low, intermediate, or high. Low-mass stars have low surface temperatures and use fuel so slowly that they may continue to fuse **hydrogen** from about 100 billion to more than 1 trillion years. Intermediate-mass stars can fuse hydrogen for billions of years, but not for as long as low-mass stars do. High-mass stars form quickly and have short lives for stars—often less than 10 million years. High-mass stars burn very hot and are blue.

Stars at various stages in their life cycle in a natural-color photomosaic (incomplete at upper left)

An aging blue supergiant casting off its outer layers

Old stars

Young stars

Stars just beginning to form

What Kind of Star Is the Sun?

   Astronomers classify the sun as an intermediate-mass **star.** Intermediate-mass stars range from about ½ of a solar mass to 8 solar masses.

   The sun is about 4.6 billion years old. It is now at the stage of its life during which it gets all its energy from reactions involving **hydrogen** in its **core.**

   The sun will stay in that phase for about another 5 billion years. Then it will expand to become a red giant (see page 46). Later on, after it has run out of fuel, it will cast off its outer layers, leaving behind a core called a white dwarf. As it cools, it will slowly fade and become a black dwarf (see page 48).

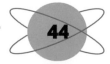

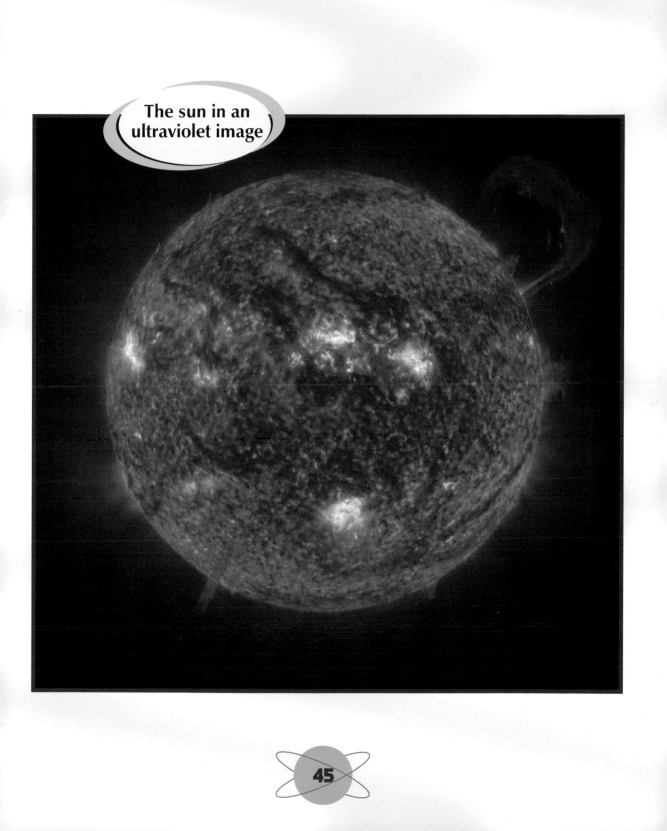

What Is a Red Giant?

A red giant is a large intermediate-mass **star** with a bright, reddish glow. When all the **hydrogen** in the **core** of an intermediate-mass star has fused into **helium,** changes rapidly occur inside the star to make it expand enormously.

As the star expands, its outer layers become cooler, so the star becomes redder. And, because the star's surface area expands greatly, the star becomes brighter. The star is now a red giant.

The red-giant stage is the first stage in which the star moves toward the end of its life cycle. This stage may last a few hundred million to a few billion years.

**Mira, a red-giant star,
in a false-color photo**

What Are a White Dwarf and a Black Dwarf?

A white dwarf and a black dwarf represent the final two stages in the life cycle of such an intermediate-mass **star** as the sun. These stages occur after the red-giant stage.

A white dwarf is a star that has burned up all of its fuel. Such a star consists mostly of the **carbon** and **oxygen** that remain at the **core** after the star has cast off its outer layers. A white dwarf is not actually white. Its color, which depends on its temperature, is violet to deep red. However, a white dwarf is too faint to be seen without a telescope.

After billions of years, a white dwarf stops shining and becomes a black dwarf. Our **universe** is so young that there are probably not yet any stars that have had time to become black dwarfs, but there should be black dwarfs in the future.

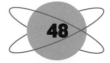

An artist's drawing of
a white dwarf

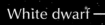 White dwarf

What Is a Supernova?

A supernova is an exploding star. It ends the life cycle of a high-mass **star.** A high-mass star is hot and blue. As it dies, the star slowly gets even hotter and swells into a bright, red supergiant. After that, it suddenly collapses and then violently explodes as a supernova.

The exploded star can become billions of times as bright as the sun before fading from view. A supernova explosion throws a large cloud of gas and dust into space, from which new stars may later form.

Astronomers classify supernovae (*supernovae* is the plural of supernova) into two types. A Type II supernova results from the death of a single, massive star. The Type I kind probably occurs in certain pairs of stars.

A supernova in a composite, false-color photo

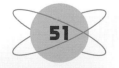

What Is a Neutron Star?

A neutron **star** is a small dense object that can be left behind after a large star explodes. A dense object has its particles packed together very tightly.

Neutron stars have a **mass** of up to 3 times that of the sun. This mass is packed into a ball with a **radius** of only about 6 to 10 miles (10 to 15 kilometers).

A neutron star is the spinning **core** that remains after a high-mass star explodes as a supernova. A neutron star is so small that its visible light is difficult to detect, but these stars also send out radio waves. Neutron stars that send out radio waves in regular pulses are called **pulsars.**

Scientists predicted the existence of neutron stars in 1938. It was not, however, until 1967 that neutron stars were actually discovered by scientists using special telescopes. These were telescopes that were able to detect radio waves.

Close-up of central area showing bright
X rays surrounding a pulsar

Bright X rays surround
a pulsar (not visible)
in an X-ray image

What Is a Black Hole?

A black hole is a region of space where **gravity** is so strong that nothing can escape from it. Black holes are invisible to **astronomers,** because not even light can escape the gravity of a black hole.

If the **core** of the **star** remaining after a supernova explosion has a mass of about three times as great as the sun's, or greater, then the core collapses. It does so in a fraction of a second, forming a black hole. All the star's mass is located at a single tiny point in its center. This center is smaller than the nucleus of an **atom.**

Although we cannot see a black hole directly, we can see its effect on stars and other objects that are drawn toward it. Scientists believe that an extremely massive black hole lies at the center of most **galaxies.**

Black holes may also produce some **radiation** that can be observed. Scientists think that gas falling into a black hole can heat up to extreme temperatures. This heat may produce jets of radiation that can be seen from Earth.

A disk of matter spirals into a black hole in this artist's conception, producing jets of radiation

What Are Binary Stars?

Binary **stars** are pairs of stars that are close together and cannot escape from each other. They hold each other captive by the force of **gravity,** and they **orbit** around each other. Most binaries are so close together that they look like single stars. Some stars appear to orbit an invisible companion that may be a black hole.

Mass transfer occurs in various forms between binary stars when their gravity is not equal. In this process, matter flows from one star to the other.

About 75 percent of all stars are binary stars. The sun is not a binary star. The closest binary star to Earth is made up of Alpha Centauri A and Alpha Centauri B. These stars are about 4.4 **light-years** away from Earth.

What Is a Brown Dwarf?

A brown dwarf is a dim object in space that has more **mass** than a **planet** but less mass than a **star.** Brown dwarfs are all about the same size as the planet Jupiter—larger than Earth but smaller than the sun— but they have 13 to 75 times Jupiter's mass.

A brown dwarf forms the same way a star does— from a huge, swirling cloud of gases and dust in space that shrinks into a ball, spins, and heats up. The warmest and brightest brown dwarfs glow a dull red and resemble low-mass stars called red dwarfs. But a brown dwarf does not have enough mass to get hot enough to become a star. Instead, it continues to shrink and then cools and fades.

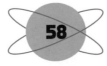

An artist's conception of a
brown dwarf being drawn
in by a star

How Do Stars and Groups of Stars Get Their Names?

Usually, if a star has a name, it has been important to people in some way. Perhaps the star is very bright in the night sky, like the star Sirius. Or, the star may be used by travelers to find their way. For example, Polaris, also called the North Star, has long been used by navigators.

For thousands of years, people have seen shapes in the stars. Some patterns have seemed to be shaped like animals, other patterns have reminded stargazers of people or objects. People have often named these groups of stars, called **constellations,** after animals or people from stories. For example, the constellation Ursa Major, meaning Great Bear, was named for an ancient Greek myth.

Today, the International Astronomical Union (IAU) is the authority that assigns names to stars. The IAU recognizes 88 constellations that cover the entire sky, most of which were named long ago. But for names of newly discovered stars, the IAU uses only letters and numbers. For example, for the star PSR J1302-6350, the letters PSR indicate that the star is a **pulsar** and what follows is a code for the star's location in the sky.

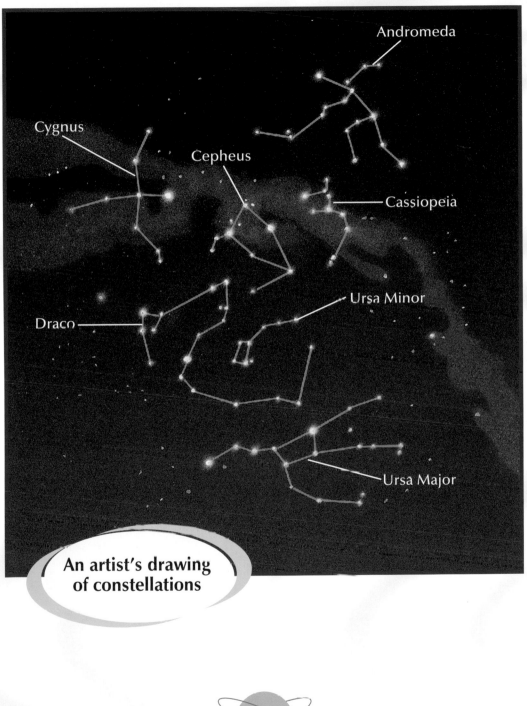

Andromeda

Cygnus

Cepheus

Cassiopeia

Ursa Minor

Draco

Ursa Major

An artist's drawing of constellations

FUN FACTS About the SUN & OTHER STARS

★ The sun has 99.8 percent of the mass in the **solar system.**

★ It takes about 250 million years for the sun to make one **orbit** around the center of the Milky Way **Galaxy.**

★ If conditions are right, you might one day see the beautifully colored lights in the sky called aurora, or the northern or southern lights. They are caused by electrically charged particles from the sun interacting with **atoms** and **molecules** from Earth's **atmosphere.** Auroras are most commonly seen very far north or very far south, near Earth's poles. But, every now and again, they can be seen closer to the equator.

★ The word *solar* comes from *sol,* the Latin word for sun. The word *star* comes from the Old English word *steorra.*

★ The light we see today from distant stars has been traveling for millions of years, so when we gaze at the stars, we're actually looking into the past!

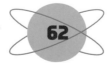

Glossary

asteroid A small body made of rock, carbon, or metal that orbits the sun. Most asteroids are between the orbits of Mars and Jupiter.

astronomer A scientist who studies stars and planets.

atmosphere The mass of gases that surrounds a planet or star.

atom One of the basic units of matter.

carbon A nonmetallic chemical element.

comet A small body made of dirt and ice that orbits the sun.

constellation A pattern of stars visible within a particular region of the night sky.

core The center part of the inside of a planet or star.

coronal mass ejection When large amounts of material from the sun's corona erupts into space.

electron A negatively charged particle that forms part of an atom.

galaxy A group of billions of stars forming one system.

gravity The effect of a force of attraction that acts between all objects because of their mass (that is, the amount of matter the objects have).

helium The second most abundant chemical element in the universe.

hydrogen The most abundant chemical element in the universe.

ion An atom or a group of atoms that has an electric charge.

Kelvin A metric unit used to measure temperatures. The Kelvin scale starts at absolute zero—the temperature at which scientists think that atoms and molecules have the least possible energy. On the Fahrenheit and Celsius scales, absolute zero is equal to −459.67 °F and −273.15 °C, respectively. From absolute zero, or 0 K, the scale rises by units of 1 Kelvin, which is equal to 1.8 Fahrenheit degrees or 1 Celsius degree.

light-year The distance that light travels in one year, equal to about 5.88 trillion miles (9.46 trillion kilometers). A jetliner traveling at a speed of 500 miles (800 kilometers) per hour would need to fly for 1.34 million years in order to travel one light-year.

magnetic field The space around a magnet or magnetized object within which its power of attraction works.

main-sequence phase The stage in the life cycle of a star at which the star gets all its energy from hydrogen fusion reactions in its core.

mass The amount of matter a thing contains.

matter The substance, or material, of which all objects are made.

molecule One of the basic units of matter.

nuclear fusion reaction A process by which two atomic nuclei join to create a new, larger nucleus; these reactions produce energy in such stars as the sun.

orbit The path that a smaller body takes around a larger body, for instance, the path that a planet takes around the sun. Also, to travel in an orbit.

oxygen A nonmetallic chemical element.

planet A large, round body in space that orbits a star. A planet must have sufficient gravitational pull to clear other objects from the area of its orbit.

plasma A form of matter, similar to gas, made up of positively charged ions and of electrons.

probe An unpiloted device sent to explore space. Most probes send data (information) from space.

pulsar An object in space that gives off regular bursts of electromagnetic radiation. Most of this radiation is in the form of radio waves. Pulsars received their name from these highly regular pulses. Scientists believe pulsars are actually neutron stars.

radiation Energy given off in the form of waves or small particles of matter.

radius Any line going straight from the center to the outside of a circle or sphere. The distance from the center of a star to its surface is a star's radius.

satellite An artificial satellite is an object built by people and launched into space, where it continuously orbits Earth or some other body.

solar flare A sudden brightening of a part of the solar atmosphere that releases a tremendous amount of energy.

solar system A group of bodies in space made up of a star and the planets and other objects orbiting around that star.

spectrum A band of visible light, or some other kind of radiation, arranged in order of wavelength. (Wavelength is the distance between successive wave crests.) A rainbow is a spectrum.

star A huge, shining ball in space that produces a tremendous amount of light and other forms of energy.

sunspot A dark, circular feature on the solar surface.

universe Everything that exists anywhere in space and time.

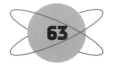

Index

For more information about the sun and other stars, try these resources:

Sun:

Secrets of the Sun, by Patricia Barnes-Svarney,
    Steck-Vaughn, 2001

The Sun, by Michael D. Cole, Enslow, 2001

The Sun, by Seymour Simon, Sagebrush, 1999

Stars:

Do Stars Have Points?, by Melvin and Gilda
    Berger, Scholastic, 1999

Fact on File Stars & Planets Atlas, by Ian Ridpath,
    Facts on File, 2005

Stars, by Seymour Simon, Sagebrush, 1999

Sun:

http://ds9.ssl.berkeley.edu/viewer/flash/flash.html

http://sohowww.nascom.nasa.gov/

http://www.jpl.nasa.gov/solar_system/sun/sun_index.html

Stars:

http://hubblesite.org/fun_.and._games/tonights_sky/

http://www.jpl.nasa.gov/stars_galaxies/